S0-BZH-523

I Can Read About

The Sun and Other Stars

Written by Richard Harris
Illustrated by Dennis Davidson

Troll Associates

Illustrations copyright © 1996 by Dennis Davidson.

Text copyright © 1996 by Troll Communications L. L. C.

Published by Troll Associates, an imprint and registered trademark of Troll Communications L. L. C.

All rights reserved. No part of this book may be reproduced or utilized in any form or by any means, electronic or mechanical, including photocopying, recording, or by any information storage and retrieval system, without written permission from the publisher.

Printed in the United States of America.

10 9 8 7 6 5 4 3 2 1

Library of Congress Cataloging-in-Publication Data
Harris, Richard, (date)
    I can read about the sun and other stars / written by
Richard Harris ; illustrated by Dennis Davidson.
    p.   cm.
  ISBN 0-8167-3634-0 (lib. bdg.) — ISBN 0-8167-3635-9 (pbk.)
  1. Stars—Juvenile literature. 2. Sun—Juvenile literature. [1. Stars. 2. Sun.]
  I. Davidson, Dennis, (date) ill. II. Title.
  QB801.7.H37   1996
  523.7—dc20   95-4211

Look up. One . . . two . . . three stars begin to blink. Then, before you know it, thousands of stars fill the nighttime sky.

But in the daytime, where do they go? In the daytime, we can see only one star—the sun. The sun is our special star.

The other stars are still in the sky. The earth turns and the sun rises. It shines brightly and brings us day. We cannot see the stars, but they are still there.

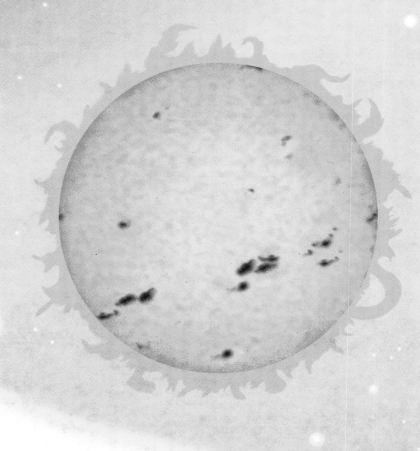

Yes, the sun is our special star.
It is a large, round ball of swirling hot gases.
And it is very important to us on Earth. The sun
gives us the heat and light we need in order to live.

The sun is very, very hot. The temperature of the outside of the sun is many thousands of degrees. The center of the sun is much hotter—about 27 million degrees Fahrenheit (15 million degrees Celsius).

The sun is the closest star to Earth. Although it is close, it is still very far away. Our special star is about 93 million miles (150 million kilometers) away.

Suppose you could jump into a rocket ship and visit the next closest star. It is called Alpha Centauri (Al-fa sent-TOR-ee). It is 26 trillion miles (42 trillion kilometers) away. Even if you could travel there, you still couldn't get very close. All stars are hot balls of gas just like the sun. Nothing can live on their fiery surfaces.

Sun

Mercury

Venus

Earth

Mars

Jupiter

The sun is the center of our solar system. There are nine planets in our solar system. Earth is the third planet from the sun. Earth only gets a small part of the sun's heat and energy. But it is just enough to make Earth a very comfortable place.

Pluto

Neptune

Uranus

Saturn

If we received any more heat, our planet would burn up.

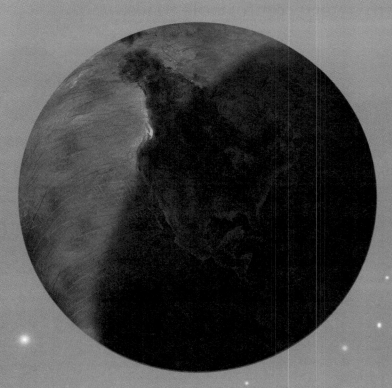

If we received any less heat, our planet might freeze.

The sun is very important to us. Long ago the Egyptians and Babylonians worshipped the sun as a god. Even then people knew that the sun was the source of light, heat, and energy for Earth.

Without the sun, we would have no rain. Plants would not grow.
There would be no food.

Without the sun, our Earth would be a cold, dry planet spinning through space.

Although the sun is so important to us, there is still a lot we don't know about it.

Scientists who study stars are called astronomers (as-TRON-uh-mers). Astronomers use special telescopes that let them study the sun without hurting their eyes. These telescopes take pictures of the sun.

Scientists know that the sun is a very lively place. There are bursts of light, swirling gases, and flames looping and leaping from the sun. There are pops and explosions.

The sun is made up mainly of a gas called hydrogen, and a small amount of a gas called helium. Both of these gases are also found on Earth.

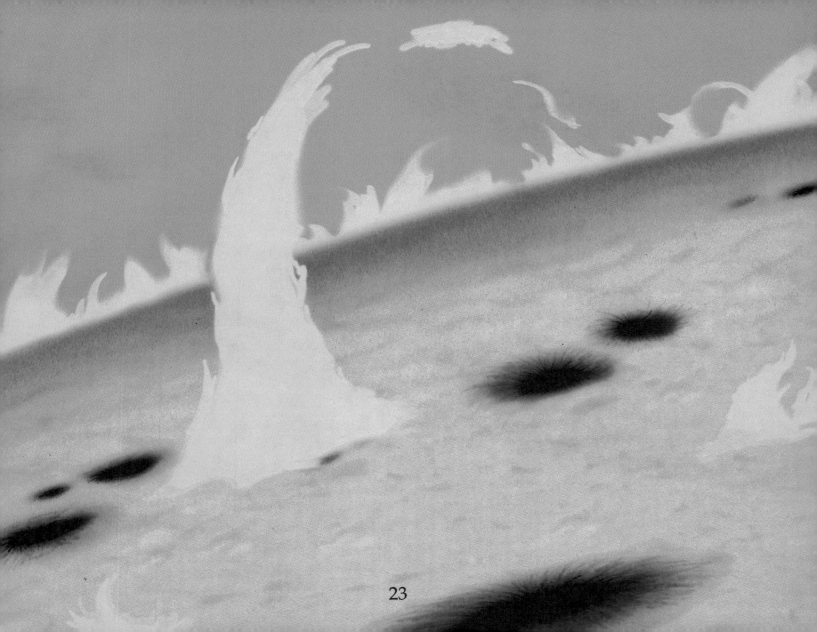

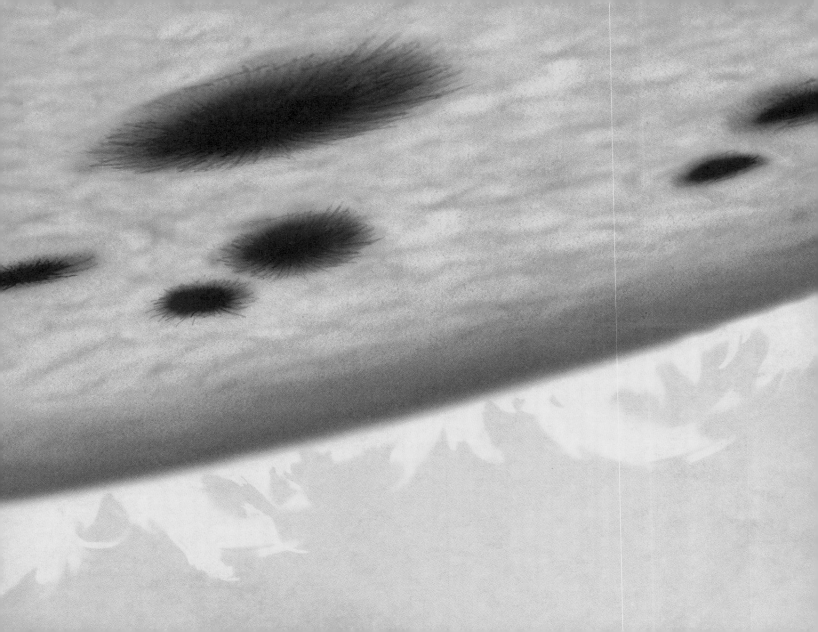

Gases on the surface of the sun are always changing . . . rising and falling all the time. Sunspots are dark spots on the sun. They may be caused by gas from the inside of the sun pushing up through the surface. Sunspots are cooler than the rest of the sun. They are sometimes 100,000 miles (161,000 kilometers) wide. Sometimes they are only a few hundred miles wide.

Scientists also study the size, brightness, and color of stars. Our sun is only a medium-sized yellow star. It is not a supergiant, or even a giant star. Still, our sun is larger than the small stars called white dwarfs.

Our sun seems big to us
because it is so close to Earth.

Our sun is more than a million times larger than Earth. Most white dwarfs are smaller than Earth. They give off a hot, white light.

No one knows how many stars are in the sky. On a clear night, you can see about three thousand stars. But there are billions of stars far out in space. Have you ever looked at the sky and wondered what is beyond the stars?

Did you know that stars come in all different kinds of colors? Some glow red and yellow. Some glow orange or blue or white. Their colors show how hot their outside temperatures are.

Sometimes, stars look pointed, but they are round . . . just like our own sun.

Sometimes, stars seem to twinkle. The twinkling is caused by air above Earth. As starlight travels toward Earth, the moving air bends the starlight, and makes it twinkle.

People have always wondered about the stars in the sky. Sometimes on a clear night, you can see a white cloud of dust far away in the distance.

When the ancient Greeks looked at these clouds, they thought these clouds looked like milk. They called them a galaxy. The Greek word for milky is galaxy. Our solar system—with the sun, planets, and stars—is part of the Milky Way Galaxy.

The Milky Way is just one galaxy moving through space. There are about 100 billion stars in the Milky Way Galaxy. By looking through a high-powered telescope, you can see another galaxy. It is called the Andromeda (An-DROM-a-da) Galaxy. It is much larger than the Milky Way Galaxy. Within the galaxies there are groups of stars that travel together. These groups are called constellations.

Long ago some people thought the constellations formed pictures in the sky. What good imaginations they had! They connected the stars with imaginary lines. And they gave the constellations names like Leo the Lion, Orion the Hunter, the Big Dipper . . .

. . . Pegasus the Winged Horse, and the Great Bear. Look up into the sky one starry night. Can you find any of these constellations?

We can tell the change of seasons by watching the constellations.
In the winter, Orion the Hunter is directly above us.

In the spring, Leo the Lion is above us.

Stars are wonderful to steer by. One star that always seems to be in the same place is the North Star, or Polaris Star. It is directly over the North Pole.

North Star

Polaris is very bright. It is sometimes the first star you see in the evening sky. Sailors use the North Star to tell direction, because they always know exactly where it is.

Sailors often use a special instrument called a sextant to focus on stars such as Polaris to determine their ship's location.

Even though there are billions of stars and galaxies spinning through space, the universe is so vast that it almost seems empty.

We know that our sun, our Earth and the other planets, and the billions of stars that make up the Milky Way Galaxy are only a small speck in space. Is anybody listening?

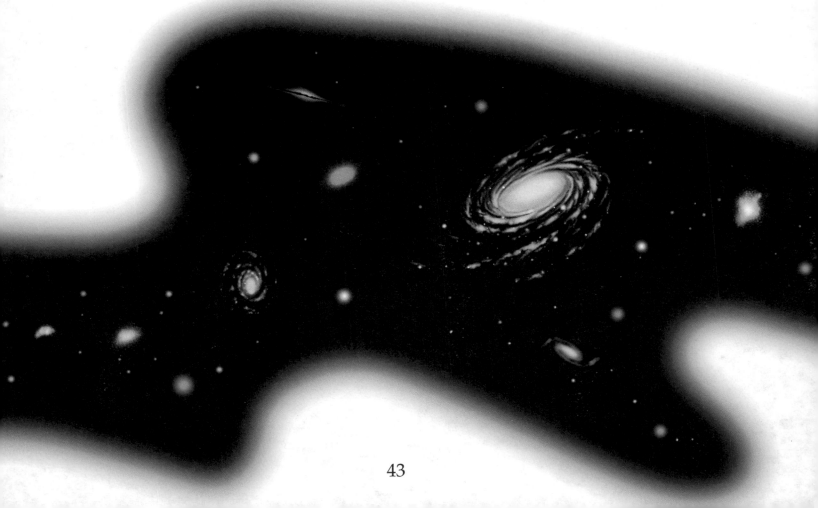

Scientists send radio signals out into space, hoping to make some kind of contact in the universe. They are always looking for new ways to discover what is beyond the eye of the most powerful telescopes on Earth.

In recent years, scientists have sent telescopes into space. One space telescope, the Hubble Space Telescope, has sent back amazing pictures of distant stars and galaxies.

As a result of pictures taken by the Hubble, some scientists and astronomers think they have discovered a new kind of star called a brown dwarf.

How many stars are in the sky? Is there life in the universe?
How big is space?

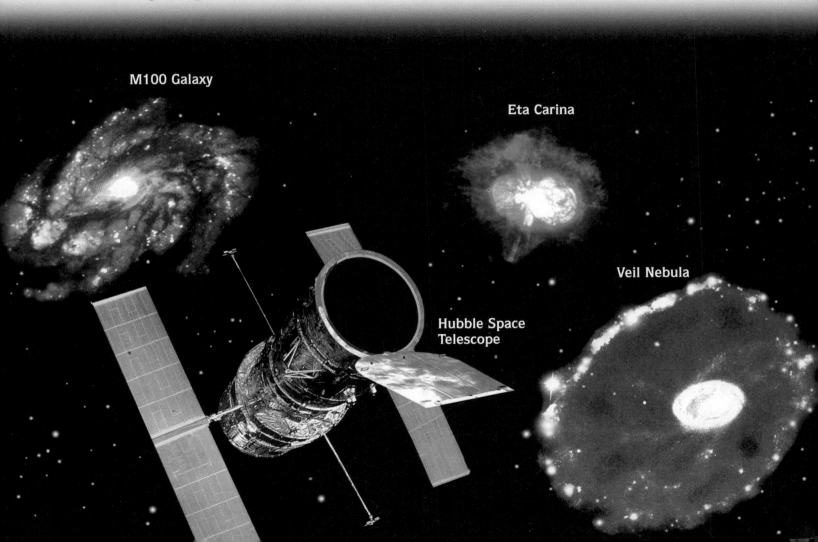

M100 Galaxy

Eta Carina

Veil Nebula

Hubble Space
Telescope

Someday we'll find out. Someday we'll look up at the stars and learn the answers. Someday we'll solve the many mysteries of space.